Working for Myself

HANDY ALL AROUND

Tana Reiff

AGS®

American Guidance Service, Inc.
Circle Pines, Minnesota 55014-1796
1-800-328-2560

Working for Myself

Beauty and the Business
Clean as a Whistle
Cooking for a Crowd
Crafting a Business
The Flower Man
The Green Team
Other People's Pets
You Call, We Haul
Your Kids and Mine

Cover Illustration: James Balkovek
Cover Design: Ina McInnis
Text Designer: Diann Abbott

Printed in the United States of America
ISBN 0-7854-1112-7 (Previously ISBN 1-56103-907-1)
Product Number 40835
A 0 9 8 7 6 5 4 3 2

CONTENTS

Chapter

CHAPTER 1

It's Not a Job

"Don't have a job, don't want a job." That's what Wayne Hiller told people when they asked what kind of job he had.

"So what do you *do*?" they'd say.

"This and that, this and that," Wayne would answer.

Those words were true. If you needed someone to paint, Wayne could do it. Need a porch light fixed? Call Wayne. Need some leaves and brush cleared from the back lot? Wayne's your man.

Sometimes he might be driving by a house and see something that needed doing. Then he'd just walk up to the front door and knock.

"I see your roof gutters are full of wet leaves," Wayne would say. "I can clean them all out for you."

More often than not, the person at the door would say, "Sure, go ahead. I've been meaning to get to that for a long time."

Wayne carried a special pad of forms. He would take a pen and write "Clean out roof gutters. $50." He'd tear off the top copy and hand it to the person. He'd stuff the other copy into his back pocket.

Then Wayne would get right to work. He'd pull just the right tools from his truck. He'd clean out that gutter until it looked like new. When he finished the job, he'd knock on the door again. He'd show the customer his work and collect his money.

Then Wayne would be on his way.

Before long he'd find another house that needed something cleaned or fixed or painted. But he didn't have a job, he would say. And he didn't want one, either. Job or no job, he was busy every day it didn't rain and some days when it did.

No one knew how much money Wayne really made. It was a lot more than anyone might have guessed. He paid his rent and electric bill every month. He paid his taxes. He bought groceries and some other things he needed. The rest of his money he put in the bank.

Wayne knew that someday he would need a new truck. He might even want to buy a house in the future. And it would be nice to have his own workshop, too, he thought. But for now, the money piled up, and Wayne kept on working.

He didn't have a *job*, though. He didn't even like to hear people say he did "odd jobs." "I know I'm odd," he would say. "But don't call it a job." That always brought a laugh.

Wayne's smile and easy way helped bring him most of his work. If Wayne came up and knocked on your door, you liked him right away. You knew by his face and manner that he was an honest, nice guy. If he had worked for your friend or neighbor, you knew he did good work. If he had worked for you before, you knew how fair he was. Wayne Hiller was easy to trust. He trusted people back, too.

It all started when Wayne was in high school. Other kids were getting jobs after school. But Wayne didn't want a job like that. He wanted to fix things around the house, that's all.

Wayne never seemed like a "go-getter." But he was, in his own way. The other kids in the neighborhood would be working in a store or a restaurant. Wayne would go around and watch people working on their homes and yards. He did yard work right along with Mrs. Wiggin, the woman who lived behind his house. That's how he learned to do yard work. He watched the old man who lived around the corner paint his house. That's how Wayne learned to paint. He watched his next-door neighbor fix toasters and radios. That's how he learned to do that kind of work.

Soon Wayne started saying to people, "I'll do that for you." He wasn't even looking for money back then. But people gave him a dollar here, a dollar there. An odd job here and an odd job there started Wayne on his way. He said you didn't have to be odd to do such work. You just had to do things right.

CHAPTER 2

A Lot to Learn

Wayne did yard work with Mrs. Wiggin for a few months. Then one day she said, "Wayne, I want to pay you."

"You don't have to do that, Mrs. Wiggin," he said.

"Well, just a little something," she said. "After all, it *is* work. People get paid for such work. You should, too."

Mrs. Wiggin gave Wayne a dollar every time he helped out. He never spent it.

Not on clothes, or CD's, or girls—or anything else.

Then one day Mrs. Wiggin handed Wayne an extra few dollars. She said, "Why don't you buy yourself a new shirt, Wayne? You should have enough money by now."

"I don't need a new shirt," Wayne said. He brushed his hand against a hole under his shirt pocket. He touched it as if he could brush it away. He couldn't, of course.

"Just a thought," said Mrs. Wiggin.

They kept on raking. A few minutes later, Mrs. Wiggin asked, "Wayne, what do you do with your money?"

"Oh, nothing," he said.

"Do you hide it away?" she asked.

"Yes. I hide it away."

"Well, if you're not going to spend it, why don't you put it in the bank? That way, it can earn some interest."

"That's a good idea," Wayne said. And that's how he began saving money in the bank. Saving had now become a habit.

Wayne also spent time with the old man who lived around the corner. Mr. Mazey's house was made of wood. He didn't want siding on his house. He liked the wood. But he had to paint it every few years. It was a big job—especially for an old guy.

Wayne said he would help Mr. Mazey paint. But the old man said he didn't want any help. Wayne asked if he could watch. Mr. Mazey said he didn't like to be watched. But he said that Wayne could hang around and keep him company.

So that's what Wayne did. He kept Mr. Mazey company. The two of them talked a little, but not much. Mostly, Wayne watched Mr. Mazey work, even if they didn't call it that.

Mr. Mazey worked very slowly. Wayne guessed that he probably moved faster when he was younger. But Wayne was glad the man worked slowly. That way,

Wayne could see everything Mr. Mazey did. It was like watching a play in slow motion. Mr. Mazey was very, very careful. Just by watching, Wayne learned every step of a painting job.

When Mr. Mazey finished the outside of the house, he began to paint the inside. Room by room, Wayne watched the old man work.

The other person Wayne spent time with was his next-door neighbor. Mr. Greer ran a small business out of his garage. He could repair just about anything people brought him. Toasters and radios were only a small part of it. Mr. Greer knew the inside of any small machine you could think of.

Mr. Greer kept all kinds of parts in his garage workshop. Some of them hung from hooks on the walls. He kept the tiny parts in a chest with little drawers. He kept big parts on a shelf.

Mr. Greer had all kinds of tools, too. He had screwdrivers and pliers and wrenches of every size. He had special tools for sanding and cutting and polishing. He had a whole shelf of glues and pastes. Another shelf was filled with nothing but boxes and jars of screws and nails.

Wayne never got tired of spending time in Mr. Greer's workshop. To him, it seemed almost like a big hardware store. Everywhere he looked, there was something interesting and useful. Coils of wire. Racks of files and chisels and saws. Tiny bottles of machine oil. Big buckets of paint and varnish and wood stains.

Mr. Greer loved having Wayne around. The man liked to talk as he worked. First he would point inside the radio or iron or toaster or whatever he was working on right then.

"Now this right here is the heart of the thing," he'd tell Wayne. "As you can see, this part is no good. But I just happen to have a good one over here. So we'll just take out this bad part and put in a new one. Then it'll be as good as new!"

Mr. Greer explained every step of every job. Wayne listened to every word. He watched everything the man did. He thought Mr. Greer was just about the smartest man in the world. He was the closest thing to a father that Wayne had ever had.

Then Mr. Greer began letting Wayne do things. At first he just gave Wayne small jobs—like tightening a screw or measuring a bit of wire. Sometimes he had Wayne clean or oil or sharpen his tools. Wayne caught on right away—and no wonder. He had seen so much already. Mr. Greer paid Wayne for his time. It wasn't much, but it was enough to make Wayne feel important.

Wayne watched Mr. Greer work out many different problems. Then Wayne got to work them out himself. Mr. Greer was always there to answer his questions along the way.

Sometimes Mr. Greer had more work than he could handle. Then he'd let Wayne take things to work on at home.

Working with Mr. Greer was how Wayne learned to fix things. In time he got very good at fixing things himself.

CHAPTER 3

One Thing Leads to Another

Wayne's handyman business started with the neighbors and grew from there. Mrs. Wiggin, Mr. Mazey, and Mr. Greer were like anyone else. They all had friends. They all had family. They told everyone they knew about Wayne.

Mrs. Wiggin had a sister across town. The sister also lived alone. She too needed help with her yard work. She had leaves to rake. She had a hedge to trim.

When Mrs. Wiggin told her about Wayne, she called him.

At the time, Wayne had just gotten out of high school. It was before he had his own truck. He walked the whole way across town to work for Mrs. Wiggin's sister.

He raked leaves and trimmed hedges there all day. By 5:00 P.M. he still wasn't finished. "I'd like to leave before it gets dark," he told Mrs. Wiggin's sister. "Is it all right if I come back tomorrow?"

"Sure," she said.

So the next day Wayne walked the whole way across town all over again. He worked until about noon. Then Mrs. Wiggin's sister said, "Do you think my doors and window frames could use a little paint?"

Wayne saw the paint chipping and peeling off the doors and window frames. "Yes, ma'am," he said. "I believe they do need some paint."

"Can you do that kind of work?" she

asked Wayne with a warm smile.

"Yes, I can," said Wayne.

Mrs. Wiggin's sister asked him to come back a third day to paint.

The next morning Wayne stopped at a paint store. He bought two gallons of paint, some sandpaper and a paintbrush. This time he decided to take the bus across town.

The paint on the doors and window frames was in bad shape. Wayne had to sand them down before he could do anything else. But by the time he finished sanding, it was too late to start painting that way.

So he came back the fourth day. It took almost all day to put a first coat on the doors and window frames.

He came back the fifth day to put on the finishing coat.

"It looks wonderful!" said Mrs. Wiggin's sister. "I feel like I'm living in a brand new house!"

Wayne was glad the woman was happy

with his work. All the way home he thought about it. He had gotten a whole week's work from one person!

Mrs. Wiggin's sister had a neighbor, Mrs. Johnson. When she saw Wayne's work, she was amazed. She thought the yard looked beautiful. She couldn't believe how perfect the paint job was. She asked for Wayne's phone number.

Mrs. Johnson called Wayne right away. She had all kinds of work for him. "I really need a handyman," she told him. That was the very first time anyone had called Wayne a "handyman." She had put a name on the work he did. He liked that.

Wayne spent three days at Mrs. Johnson's home. She was getting ready for summer. She paid Wayne to paint her lawn chairs. She also had a garden to dig and a hedge to trim.

That week Mrs. Johnson told her brother-in-law about Wayne. It so happened that the man lived in Wayne's neighborhood. So when Wayne worked for him, he didn't have far to walk. Wayne always enjoyed walking to work. He liked to look at people's yards and gardens. He liked to look for jobs that he could do on people's houses.

Still Wayne began to daydream about owning a truck. There were only two problems with that. First, he was pretty sure that he didn't have enough money to buy one. And second, he had never learned how to drive.

Wayne had never had a good reason to learn to drive. He never went far from home. But he could see that a truck would be handy for hauling around tools and paint, cans and a ladder. Wayne was surprised that some people did not own a ladder. So he thought it would be good to always carry one with him.

Mr. Mazey had a son whose house needed some painting. Before, Mr. Mazey had always done that for his son. Since he retired from his job, he had plenty of time for such projects. But this time he said he was getting too old. He told his son about Wayne, even though he had never seen Wayne work.

Wayne walked to Mr. Mazey's son's house. On the way, he spotted an old pickup truck parked on the street. In the truck's back window was a sign that said, "For Sale. Best Offer."

"I wonder what an old truck like that is worth?" Wayne said to himself. He decided to knock on the door and talk to the owner.

"It runs all right," said the man. "But the bed is pretty rusted out."

Wayne saw the holes in the truck bed. As the man talked, Wayne was thinking of ways to patch up the holes.

"This old truck has done a good job for me. But I really don't need it anymore. Now I just want to get rid of it," said the man. "I'll take $300."

Wayne knew he had at least that much money in the bank. He asked the man to take the sign off the truck. He told him that he'd come back the next day with the money.

The next morning Wayne stopped at the bank. Then he hurried off to buy his "new" old truck. Now all he had to do was fix it up. No problem. Oh, yes, he also had to learn to drive it.

CHAPTER 4

Getting It in Writing

At first Wayne never wrote anything down on paper. If someone wanted him to do some work, he just did it. Then he took the money and went on his way.

Then one time he got burned. Well, he wasn't really *burned*, like with fire. He was burned over money. It happened not long after Wayne starting driving. He had asked Mr. Greer to teach him.

"Don't you want to learn how to drive

a *car* first?" Mr. Greer had asked him. "Cars are easier than trucks."

"No," Wayne said. "I don't think I'll ever have any use for a car. Just teach me on the truck."

So Mr. Greer went along with Wayne in the rusty old truck. The engine wasn't too bad for its age. That much of the truck had been kept up. Wayne already knew the body and bed were in bad shape. He worked on fixing the holes in the truck bed. But the gear box was a bigger problem. When Wayne went to shift gears, it sounded like the whole truck was ripping apart.

Mr. Greer not only taught Wayne how to drive. He also taught him how to fix a gear box.

Wayne took to driving the truck like he took to fixing things. It was the driving *book* that gave him a hard time. The book had information about the state's laws on driving. Before you could get a license, you had to pass a written test. The test asked questions about the laws. Some of the questions were hard. And, of course, you had to pass an "on the road" driving test, too.

Every night, Mr. Greer asked Wayne questions from the book. Often the two of them were working together in Mr. Greer's garage at the same time. Wayne said they were killing two birds with one stone.

One night Mr. Greer said, "Wayne, I think you're ready to take the driving test. Do you want to go over to the motor bureau tomorrow?"

"I guess so," said Wayne. He wasn't as sure of himself as Mr. Greer was. But he thought if Mr. Greer said he was ready, then maybe he was.

Wayne passed both the written and the road test on his first try. He was really happy. To celebrate, his mother made him a nice dinner that night. Wayne wanted to take her for a ride in the truck. But she said it would be too bumpy. She would rather stay home, she said.

A few days later, Wayne drove his truck to a part of town he'd never been in before. He parked his truck at the curb and starting walking from door to door, looking for work.

At one house, a woman answered the door. "We have tree branches hanging over the neighbor's yard," she told Wayne. "Can you cut back those branches for me?"

As always, Wayne got right to work. As always, he didn't write anything down on paper. He just told the woman a price, she agreed, and that was that.

Wayne set up his ladder. He trimmed the branches and put them in the truck. Later he'd take them to a guy who would cut them up and sell them for firewood. He paid Wayne a few dollars for bringing him the branches. Then Wayne went back to the woman to get paid.

"You can get your money from my neighbor, OK?" the woman said. "He was the one who wanted the branches out of the way in the first place. He can just pay for it, too."

"I can't do that, ma'am," Wayne said. "You're the one who asked me to do the work. It's *your* yard."

"Well, then, take me to court," said the woman. "I'm not paying you." She shut the door in his face.

Wayne didn't want to take anyone to court. He didn't want to make a fuss. Besides, he knew he didn't have a leg to stand on. He had nothing written down on paper to prove that he'd been hired. He knew he'd never see any money for trimming those branches.

From that day on, Wayne began writing things down. He bought a pad of two-part forms. When someone wanted him to do some work, he wrote down what the work was. Below that, he wrote a price. Then he signed his name and asked the customer to sign, too. He gave the person one copy of the form, and he kept the other part. That way there was no mistake about what he was doing, how much it would cost, and who should pay him.

About this time Wayne saw that being a handyman could be a real business. He still didn't look at it as a job. He didn't get up and go to the same place every day. He didn't get a paycheck every week. But being a handyman was work that earned money. That made it a business.

CHAPTER 5

Getting Down to Business

Wayne got even more serious about his business when his mother died.

She had been feeling sick for only a few days. It started out like a cold. Everyone gets colds. But Wayne's mother didn't get better. Pretty soon she could hardly get out of bed.

"I think you should call the doctor, Mom," Wayne told her. "I'm worried."

"Oh, don't worry. It's just a cold," she

kept saying. She didn't like doctors.

Wayne started thinking it was more than a cold. He thought about calling the doctor himself. But his mother had always been able to take care of herself— and him, too. So he let it go.

Then one morning, as she tried to get out of bed, she passed out. Wayne called for an ambulance right away. He rode with her to the hospital.

By the time a doctor saw Wayne's mother, it was too late. The doctors did all they could for her. But she was already seriously ill. She died in the hospital two days later.

Wayne had never thought about not having his mother around. He couldn't remember his father—he had died when Wayne was still a baby. But his mom had always been there. She cooked for him and cleaned the house and paid the bills. Now it was all on his shoulders.

That's when Wayne began thinking more about what he charged for his work. Until now he would look over a job and pull a price out of his head. This kind of work was worth so much. That kind of work was worth so much. He didn't think too much about it.

But when his mother died, Wayne saw how much money was needed every month. If he couldn't come up with that much, he wouldn't be able to stay in the house.

"You need to bring home a certain amount of money for each hour you work," Mr. Greer explained. "And you need to put in at least 30 paid hours every week."

"That's a lot," Wayne said. "Right now I spend a lot of time just going from place to place."

"Let me tell you about how to figure time and materials," said Mr. Greer. "It's a way to bill for your work."

Mr. Greer explained that Wayne should count the time he spent getting to and from a job. He should add that time to the hours he spent doing the work. Then he should multiply the number of hours by how much he needed to earn for every hour of his time.

For some jobs Wayne had to buy materials, such as paint or a new storm door. Mr. Greer said he should be sure to add in those costs, too.

To give Wayne some practice, Mr. Greer made up an imaginary painting job. He tried to make it just like a real one. Together he and Wayne figured out a price for the job.

"That seems a little high to me," Wayne said. "I think some people hire me because I don't charge much."

"Don't forget, you have to cover the cost of tools and your truck, too," Mr. Greer said. "You won't stay in business if you don't get back what you put out."

"I see what you mean," Wayne said.

"There's another way you can do better, too," Mr. Greer said. "It's about time you went downtown and got yourself a contractor's license."

"What's that?" Wayne asked.

"You get a license from the city," Mr. Greer said. "That makes you a real contractor. In some states you have to take a big test to get a contractor's license. In this state you just have to fill out the forms. When you get your license, you can buy parts and materials at a lower price. Then you can charge your customers the full price, like a store would."

That sounded pretty good to Wayne.

"And you won't believe what you can find in a scrap yard!" Mr. Greer said, laughing. "Somebody throws something out because it doesn't work anymore. But inside, most of the parts might be just as good as new!"

"That's great," said Wayne. "But I don't know. I think I'm getting in kind of deep here."

"No one ever said that running a business would be easy," said Mr. Greer.

"But you'll be fine. You know what you're doing. And when you don't—you'll work it out. You just need to make sure that you get paid for everything you do. That's the most important thing."

"I'm not trying to get rich," said Wayne. "I'm not trying to live the high life or anything like that. I just want to make ends meet, you know?"

"Don't we all?" Mr. Greer laughed. "Don't we all."

So Wayne got himself a contractor's license.

The very next day, he dropped in at the Golden Years Club. The group met downstairs in a church. The room was full of square tables. At every table sat four senior citizens playing cards. Wayne went right in and started saying hello to people. He asked if anyone needed any work done around their homes. One woman asked if Wayne could put a new tub in her washing machine. "But I can't pay more than 20 dollars," she said.

Wayne wasn't sure he should do the job for 20 dollars. He didn't want to get underpaid for his work. But if he marked up the price of the part, the job might be worth his time. "What kind of washer do you have?" he asked. "The model number would help me out."

Wayne went to an appliance store to buy the part. "I need a tub for this model of washer," he said. "I'm a contractor," he added. He showed the man his license.

The salesperson wrote up Wayne's order. He took 15 percent off the bill. Wayne put the tub into the woman's washing machine. It worked like new. Wayne charged the woman the full price for the tub. He made what he had to make on the job.

CHAPTER 6

Working Alone

Wayne always enjoyed working with Mr. Greer. He always learned something from being around him.

Sometimes Wayne and Mr. Greer helped each other. Mr. Greer would often say, "Hold this for a minute, will you?" Wayne would hold something in place while Mr. Greer worked on it with both of his hands.

When Wayne worked at someone's

home, though, he worked alone. At times he thought to himself, "Boy, I wish I had three hands." But he had only two, so he worked out ways to make the best of them.

He always carried three things with him—a rubber cord, a clamp, and a string. These things always came in handy at one time or another.

Like the time he put in a new stair post for a man from the Golden Years Club. Wayne bought the post already made. All he had to do was cut it to the right size. Then he had to use a level to make sure that he put it in straight up and down. But he couldn't hold the post, the rail, and the level all at one time.

That's where the rubber cord came in handy. Wayne tied the level to the post. Then he lifted the stair rail into place with both hands. As he kept his eye on the level, he set the post straight.

The clamp was also very helpful. "You'll find a hundred uses for this thing!" the man at the building supply store had said. It didn't take Wayne long to see how true that was.

The clamp had soft pads on its jaws, so it wouldn't damage any surface. Wayne could clamp a board onto a table or another board with just one hand. With the other hand he could hammer in the nails. Before long Wayne didn't know how he had ever worked without that clamp.

He used the string for all kinds of things. One time he used it to help him round the corners of a new kitchen countertop. Wayne needed a curved line to follow when he was cutting. To draw this line he tied the string around the tip of a pencil. First he marked the string one foot from the pencil. Then he marked the backside of the counter one foot from both sides and the end. Next Wayne held the string at the one-foot mark on the mark on the counter. Finally, he pulled the string taut with the pencil and drew a perfectly round line exactly where he needed it. When he did the same thing at the other end of the counter, that part of the job was done.

Even with the tricks he had learned, Wayne still ran into jobs he couldn't do at all. He knew how to do some plumbing and electrical work. It was just that his contractor's license wouldn't let him. In his state, you had to have a plumber's license or an electrician's license to do those kinds of jobs.

One time Wayne was putting up new drywall in a bathroom. The woman said, "Wayne, can you do one more thing while you're here? Could you fix the toilet? I don't know what's wrong with it. It just runs and runs."

"Sorry," Wayne said. "You'll have to call a plumber. I don't have a license to do that kind of work."

"I see," said the woman.

Wayne was painting the drywall when he started thinking. "If I could hook up with a plumber, I could put in whole bathrooms—and kitchens, too!" he said to himself.

Wayne kept thinking about it. There *must* be a plumber out there who would like to hook up with a handyman. Together, they could give people all-in-one deals. And they could both make more money.

Wayne didn't know a plumber, though. He didn't know many people at all. He didn't even know where to begin to find a good plumber.

Then one day he went to the building supply store. There he heard a man talking to a clerk. "Do you know a good drywall man?" he asked.

The salesclerk pointed to Wayne. "Yes, this guy here comes in for drywall sometimes," he said. The man turned to Wayne. "What do you do?" he asked.

"This and that," Wayne said.

"Are you any good with drywall?" the man asked.

"Sure," said Wayne.

"I'm a plumber," the man said. "I'm putting in a new bathtub. But the shower wall is rotted. The bathroom needs all new drywall. And my regular drywall man got hurt the other day."

"I'll come over and take a look at it," said Wayne.

The plumber's name was Quang. He didn't speak English very well. At first Wayne had a little trouble understanding him. But Wayne went to see the job. Right away he could see what a great plumber this Quang was. And Quang watched as Wayne explained how he would do the drywall job. He saw that Wayne knew what *he* was doing, too.

Wayne had to laugh. He had been looking for a plumbing subcontractor. Now *he* was a subcontractor for the plumber.

Wayne and Quang began doing more and more jobs together. Quang did the plumbing. Wayne did everything else but the electrical work.

Wayne and Quang helped each other in other ways, too. Every now and then they carried heavy things together. They held things in place for each other. Four arms were always better than two. And they talked about their job problems, too. Two heads were always better than one. Over time, Wayne and Quang got to be friends.

C H A P T E R   7

Like a Snowball

"Don't you ever call that other drywall man anymore?" Wayne asked Quang one day. "Whatever happened to him?"

"He's out of work," Quang said. "He hurt his back real bad. And he didn't have insurance. Can you believe that? It's *crazy* not to have insurance!"

Wayne didn't have any insurance, either. But when he heard Quang's story, he quickly went out and got some. The insurance would pay for any damage he might cause on a job. It would pay his doctor bills if he ever got hurt. And it would even pay him enough to live on for a while if he couldn't work.

Once in a while people would still ask Wayne to do some plumbing. So he worked out a deal with Quang. Wayne would send the business to Quang. Quang would do the job. Then he would give Wayne 15 percent of what he made on the job.

"This is like getting paid for doing nothing," Wayne said.

"Not really," Quang said. "To me, it's like buying an ad in the paper. The ad brings me business. When you send me work, *you* are my ad. It's worth it to me to pay you 15 percent."

"I guess that's right," Wayne said. He started thinking that he wouldn't mind getting work from Quang, too. But he didn't like the idea of paying to get work. He had never bought an ad. He had never spent a cent to get work, except to put gas in the truck and go out looking.

Soon Quang started telling people to call Wayne for certain jobs. Wayne couldn't turn down good work. So he began to pay Quang 15 percent of what he made on those jobs. He didn't mind as much as he thought he would. The work helped keep him busy.

One time Wayne and Quang were working together on a kitchen. When Wayne tore out the old wall, he saw how bad the old wiring was.

"This room needs new wiring," he said to Quang. "Do you happen to know a good electrician?"

"You don't know *anybody*, do you?" Quang said, laughing. "Yeah, I know a good electrician. His name is Kurt. Do you think we should call him?"

"I'll talk to the customer first," Wayne said. "But I can't just go ahead and put new drywall over this wiring. It would never pass the city's code."

Wayne showed the customer the bad wiring. "See this wire? It's almost bare," Wayne explained. "Now, I don't mean to scare you. But, to me, this looks like a fire waiting to happen."

The woman didn't need to hear anymore. "Go ahead!" she said. "Call the electrician!"

That's how Wayne got to know Quang's friend Kurt. Before long Wayne didn't know what he had ever done without Kurt. He kept running into jobs that needed an electrical subcontractor. Kurt was always glad to sub for him.

Still, Wayne did most of his work alone. And that was fine with him. Sometimes, though, he ran into things he didn't know how to do.

It was spring. Wayne was doing a yard clean-up for a young working couple. They asked him if he could also fix the patio out back. The concrete was cracked and it needed a patch here and there.

Wayne didn't want to say he could do

something when he couldn't. Yet he knew himself well. More and more, he could look over a new kind of job and work out a way to do it. So he said, "Sure, I'll patch your patio. Just give me a day or two."

Kurt was working on a new house that was just going up. Another guy was putting in a patio there. So Wayne went over there to take a look.

"How do you patch an old patio?" Wayne asked the man.

The man talked as he worked. He told Wayne what he needed to buy to do the job. He showed him how to mix the stuff. He showed him how to put it on, and how to smooth it out. Wayne watched very closely. Then he did everything the man showed him.

As he patched the couple's patio, Wayne started thinking to himself. He thought about what being a handyman really is. For some reason he had never spelled it out before. A handyman is a person who likes work to be different every day. A handyman is a person who wants to give something a try even if he doesn't know how. And a handyman is a person who likes to learn new things all the time.

CHAPTER 8

Over the Line

Wayne didn't need any more work when Kurt called him that night. He was busy enough. But there were problems with the house Kurt was working on. He had to talk to Wayne.

"These people want to be in their house in three weeks," Kurt said. "The way it's going, we're not going to make it. I told the general contractor he needs one more person to do all the odd jobs. He said that

I could call you."

"Boy, I'm pretty busy," Wayne said.

"Can you put off your other work for three weeks?" Kurt asked. "This is three full weeks of work. You can start tomorrow. What do you say?"

Wayne thought about all the work he had lined up. He was sure that some of it could wait.

"Can I have the weekend and two days?" Wayne asked Kurt. "I can do what I have to do in those four days. After that I'm with you."

"Sounds good to me. I think we've got a deal," Kurt said.

So Wayne worked his tail off for the next four days. And that was after he had already put in a full five-day week.

On Saturday, he worked at four different places. He didn't quite finish his job at the last house.

On Sunday he worked from seven in the morning until seven at night at one place. Then he went back and finished up the job from Saturday. He got home at 11:00 P.M.

On Monday, he painted in the morning and did yard work until dark.

On Tuesday, he thought he couldn't get out of bed. But he did—and he worked until dark all over again.

He didn't have time to work for Mr. Greer at all. He hadn't even seen his next-door neighbor for more than two weeks now.

On Wednesday morning, Wayne got out of bed bright and early. He was sore and tired from working nine long days in a row. But he ate a good breakfast and climbed into his truck.

Wayne knew the truck was on its last legs. He knew he should have done some work on it. But he had never found the time to do it.

Wayne put his foot on the gas—and CRASH! The gas pedal went right through the rusty old floor. "Talk about pedal through the metal!" Wayne said, laughing. He pulled the pedal up and tried driving with it hanging on like that.

Wayne was about halfway to the new house when the truck stopped dead. He pulled it over and got out to take a look. He lifted the hood. This truck was going nowhere.

Wayne got his toolbox out of the back. He picked up a few of the larger tools. Then he walked the rest of the way to the new house.

He was an hour late. He was afraid that would make Kurt look bad for getting someone who showed up so late. But the general contractor was just glad to see him.

Wayne went right to work in the kitchen. He hung some cabinets. Then he laid a new counter. The tile man was coming in the afternoon. Wayne had to hurry up and finish before the man got there.

Wayne was using an electric sander to smooth off the counter. But he was moving too fast. His eyes were open, but he wasn't really awake. He had only one row left to sand when the sander slipped. It caught him in the chest.

Wayne fell to his knees. "Kurt!" he called. "You better come here." His voice wasn't very loud. Kurt didn't hear him.

Wayne called for help again. Kurt still didn't hear him. But just then he happened to walk into the kitchen.

"What the . . . !" Kurt cried out.

"Just take me to the hospital," Wayne said in a weak voice.

Wayne thought he would never have to use his insurance. He never thought he would need it. But that day, and for the next three weeks, he was very glad that he had it. The insurance covered most of the doctor bills. It also paid Wayne a little bit for every day he couldn't work.

Those three weeks were supposed to be three full weeks of work on the new house. Instead, they were three long weeks of pain and watching TV.

It did give Wayne more time with Mr. Greer, though. That was nice. It also gave him time to start looking for a new truck. That was fun.

CHAPTER 9

Signs of Growth

The old truck wasn't even worth keeping for parts. Wayne towed it down to the junk yard and said good-bye.

The new pickup he bought was really new. He got a good deal on it because it was last year's model.

Because of the accident, Wayne missed out on the new house job. When he was ready to work again, Kurt and Quang didn't have any jobs for him. He had to go back to knocking on doors. At least it was fun to ride around in the new truck. The paint job was so shiny that the sun bounced off the hood into Wayne's eyes. On a really bright, sunny day, he had to wear sunglasses.

After the time off, though, it wasn't only the truck that was different. *Everything* seemed different. Maybe it was those three weeks of rest. Maybe Wayne had a clearer head now. He didn't know. Whatever the reason, he had come up with a new way of looking at things.

He first noticed it when he was working on a roof gutter. He had worked on roof gutters many times before. This one looked no different. It was full of leaves. Wayne cleaned them out, just as he always did. He did have some trouble getting around the roof. There were tree branches poking out at different spots along the way.

As hard as it was, Wayne got the leaves out. Then it started to rain. It wasn't just a few drops. It really poured. "Let's see how your gutter works," Wayne said to the man of the house.

The rain should have washed through the gutters and down the spouting. Some of it did. But it looked as if some water was coming *through* the gutter. Wayne wasn't sure if the gutter was leaking or if there was just too much rain.

The rain let up. Wayne looked at the gutter again. Now the problem was clear. "It's leaking, all right," Wayne told the man. He counted four holes.

"Do we need a new gutter?" the man asked.

"I don't think you do," said Wayne. "The gutter is in pretty good shape for now. But you *do* need some patches."

"Fine," said the man. "How much will it cost?"

Wayne told him. "Here's the thing, though," he heard himself say. "See those tree branches hanging over? They're poking the holes in the gutter. I think we need to trim back those trees. If we don't, you'll just get more holes again."

Wayne's voice was strong. He sounded as if he knew what he was talking about. He *did* know what he was talking about. The man paid Wayne to trim the tree branches.

When Wayne finished that job, he met Quang at the local diner. They began talking about their work. They talked not only about *how* to fix things, but *why* they needed to be fixed. Wayne had never done that before.

The next day something else happened that made Wayne think. He gave a woman a price to hang a new storm door.

"That's too much," the woman said.

Wayne thought again about the price. Hanging a storm door always took longer than people expected. He added up the hours in his head. Then he added what he could make on the door itself. Maybe he could give the woman the door for what he paid for it. No, that would not give him enough. His price was fair. This time he decided to hold his ground. He knew he could find other work if this woman wouldn't pay his price.

"Sorry," Wayne said. "That's my price."

"Oh, all right," the woman said with a little smile. "I thought it was worth a shot. Go ahead and get to work."

On the way home, Wayne stopped to give someone a price on fixing some kitchen cabinets. He could see that it would take almost seven hours. That was less than a whole day. Yet that wouldn't leave enough time to do any other work that day. So the price Wayne gave was for a full day of work.

The people asked Wayne when he could start the job.

"Day after tomorrow," he said. "But I'd like to take that one cabinet with me. I can get a head start on it in my workshop at home."

Wayne wished that he really did have a good place of his own to work on the cabinet. He didn't. He still paid rent on the house he had shared with his mother. That house belonged to his landlord. He couldn't build a workshop there. So that night, as always, he took his work over to Mr. Greer's garage. He carefully set up the cabinet on the long workbench. Mr. Greer greeted him with a big smile.

"Hi, Wayne. What's new?" Mr. Greer asked him.

"To tell the truth, *a lot* is new," Wayne said. He told Mr. Greer about the gutter leaks and about sticking to his prices. He said that he had reached a new way of thinking about his work. He could feel it in his bones.

These days he wasn't just fixing things. He was finding and fixing the *real* problems behind them. It seemed that he could always either work things out or find someone who could. What's more, he was making sure he got *paid* for doing things right.

"I always knew you had what it takes,

son," said Mr. Greer. "Listen. I've been meaning to talk to you about something. I know you've got this cabinet to do, but this is . . . well, it's important. Do you have a minute?"

CHAPTER 10

Looking Ahead

"I'm not getting any younger," Mr. Greer began. "My wife has been gone for ten years now. It's getting harder and harder for me to keep up the house and all. So I've been thinking about selling the place. I wanted to offer it to you first."

Wayne's eyes lit up. "Wow," he said. "Are you going to sell the workshop, too?"

"Goes with the house," Mr. Greer said, smiling. "It's an all-in-one deal."

They started talking price. Mr. Greer took out a book that showed house payments at different interest rates. He showed Wayne just how much he would have to pay each month at today's rates.

"Do you think you could come up with that much money?" Mr. Greer asked.

"It's pretty close to what I'm paying in rent," said Wayne.

"Do you want to try to buy my house?" Mr. Greer asked.

"Oh, boy, *do* I!" said Wayne, with a big smile. He had never dreamed of such a thing.

Mr. Greer helped Wayne work things out. Together they went to different banks until they had worked out a fair deal. The whole thing took almost two months to set up. Then one day they signed some papers. Mr. Greer's house, garage, and most of his tools and parts now belonged to Wayne. He didn't buy Mr. Greer's business. He didn't want to be in the workshop all the time. He only wanted the workshop for when he needed to fix something.

Mr. Greer sold some of his personal things at a yard sale. Wayne helped him pack the rest.

Then a big van came to move Mr. Greer into an apartment across town. Wayne saw the van pull up in front of the house. All of a sudden it hit him that Mr. Greer wouldn't be next door anymore. He felt sad—like when his mother died. He didn't think about how much he would miss Mr. Greer until the time came.

Now he couldn't find the words to tell Mr. Greer how he really felt. "Can I come visit you?" was all he said.

"I'll be looking for you," Mr. Greer said. "Come by any time."

A few days later Quang and Kurt helped Wayne move in next door.

"Good house," said Kurt. "You're lucky to have it. How did you get rich enough to buy a house?"

Wayne just smiled. Kurt knew the

answer to his own question. He knew Wayne was making good money and spending very little.

Then Quang said he had to get out of his apartment very soon. "It's a big house you've got," Quang said. He wondered if Wayne might want someone to move in and pay him rent.

Since his mother died, Wayne had become used to living alone. But he got along fine with Quang. A little rent money would help. So he told Quang they had a deal.

Wayne and Quang didn't get in each other's way. They both worked long hours. Neither one was home much. If Wayne was around, he was usually working on something out in the workshop anyway.

One time Wayne, Quang, and Kurt were all working together at the same new house. Wayne thought he might get tired of seeing Quang, but he didn't. At home, Quang just sort of floated by now and then. He never made any trouble.

Soon after that new house job, Quang got married and moved out of the house. When Wayne's mother had died, Mr. Greer was next door. When Mr. Greer moved out, Quang moved in. Now when Wayne was at home, there was no one else around. For the first time, he was really alone.

Wayne didn't feel all that lonely, though. He was always out working or looking for work. There was always someone to talk to, it seemed.

Now Wayne thought about what he would do next. Before, there had always been something to work for. A truck. A new truck. A new tool. Better work. Bigger problems to work out. Buying a house. His own workshop.

Now, Wayne wasn't sure what his goals should be. Maybe he would try to do only those jobs he liked the best. Maybe he would put sides on the bed of his pick-up. Maybe he would start to have a life outside of his work. He began to think of getting married and having a family someday.

Still, if someone happened to ask Wayne what he was up to these days, he'd say what he always said: "Don't have a job, don't want a job."

And if someone asked him, "What do you do?" he'd give his usual answer.

"This and that," Wayne would say. "This and that."